Date_____19____

M_____

Address_____

Reg. No.	Clerk	Account Forward		
1				
2	Sad-Faced Men	HC		50
3				
4	fax			3
5				
6				
7				.53
8				
9				
10				
11				
12				
13				
14				
15	561 - 4			

Your Account Stated to Date – If Error Is Found Return at Once
STYLE 1200

Sad-Faced Men

William Logan

SAD-FACED MEN

DAVID R. GODINE · BOSTON
A Godine Poetry Chapbook
Fourth Series

First published in 1982 by
DAVID R. GODINE, PUBLISHER, INC.
306 Dartmouth Street
Boston, Massachusetts 02116

Library of Congress Cataloging in Publication Data

Logan, William, 1950-
   Sad-faced men.
   (A Godine poetry chapbook; 4th ser.)
   I. Title
PS3562.O4449S2   811'.54   80-83947
ISBN 0-87923-365-6

Acknowledgments: *American Review* (We Abandon the Gods
on Our First Evening Together), *Georgia Review* (An Ode),
The Nation (Observing Whales Through Binoculars; Travel
Report), *The New Yorker* (Ice; The Lizard in His Medium;
Maelstrom; The Mantis; She Arrives at Night, Unexpected),
North American Review (The Misbegotten), *Poetry* (Medusae;
Mise en Scène; The Moth Disturbs the Night; The Object;
Three Lives; Totenlieder), and *Sewanee Review* (Children;
Dream of Dying; Sheep; Tatiana Kalatschova).

The author wishes to thank the Corporation of Yaddo, the
Millay Colony for the Arts, the MacDowell Colony, and the
Ingram Merrill Foundation. The Graywolf Press published
six of these poems in a chapbook entitled *Dream of Dying*.

Printed in the United States of America

for Debora Greger

'You sad-fac'd men,...
Oh, let me teach you how to knit again
This scattered corn into one mutual sheaf,
These broken limbs again into one body.'

Titus Andronicus

Contents

Deception Island

It provides an excellent harbor
but occasionally the water boils.
—*The New York Times*

A bird-like man waits for the
Windows to clear. What will be there?
Natives dancing their unrepeatable dances.

A new species of tapir wandering
Up from the valley. Perhaps only a river,
Opal and blue—on which English swans

Hover as if at rest and at flight—
Moving its mirror toward open sea.
A postcard shows a northern snow and

Men surrounding a clapboard house
Where icicles lean on lines of light.
His coffee cools near an unfinished meal

In whose palette he finds unlikely
Attractions, excisions in a
Country of white. A tablecloth, a sky,

Spreads from one white horizon to another.
This is Antarctica. The bay in the drowned
Volcano bubbles and dies. The penguins

Run on this ice with their awkward feet.
When the sun reaches the top of the Spanish tower,
A parade of torches will begin,

Each woman lost in a mask of indigenous red.
She represents what blinds and what forgets,
The tropic sun that might rise anywhere.

1

Children

All night, though dead, they stir.
All night toward an unknown invitation
The children reach, like boats
Toward open sea, but are moored against it.
They test their tethers. They rock
And rock in a bloodless sleep. After fierce winds,
The roots of thrown trees lie wormy and exposed,
As if the dead had heaved the close earth.

All night we seem to hear their breathings
And longings, a shattered colonnade around us.
We have our silence. What you cannot express
Is subject to eruptions of nature: you anger
In the steady rolling of our mutual blood.
You are angered that we have no children. We have
An impossible genealogy, each of us a child
To the other.

Under a summer storm pasted to the sky,
You remain the only landmark worth going toward,
Or staying from. Children would marry us
Together, as captives fetter captors,
Yet wish to escape them. In the ground now
Around the house, their arms strain toward the
    windows,
Toward our silent invitations: what
Outside ourselves relieves an absence within.

In Sleep

Clouds accumulate and a woman sleeps sunless,
Her legs moving beneath the cotton sheets
With the warmed night of summer.

Her forehead, sharp from dreaming, relaxes
And she rises from bed, toward the light
Fixtures and plastered ceiling, through the oak beams

And webbed attic, through the slate roof, past
The antenna, the tangible chimney,
Into the air. The trees are green complexions

In the green background, the birds dark below her.
She is leaving, and when the earth's limits
Appear, the sky arcs faintly, a band of air.

The stars madden, and satellites hum silently
Where no sound can awaken a sleeper. She dreams
A language which cannot trouble her, a vocabulary

Without voice. She has forgotten the ugly grammar,
The deformed sentences. She has forgotten
The irregularities of memory, the unknown knowns,

The can-no-longer-remembers, the slow
        impeachment
Of experience. She rises, stunned and serene,
Toward the promise of nothing.

The Object

Consider the tears
Of a statue: made of wood, not water,
They neither swell nor move, but week
By week remain an object

Of the steady, almost cruel
Gaze of tourists. For such gazes, no tax
Could suffice, as if a monetary tax
Could justify such tears

Or make stares less cruel.
Any lake, any body of water
Makes us the object
Of our own admiration, our own weak

Tendencies expressed in the weak
Reflection of light at dawn or sunset, a tax
On the eyes—we do not object,
Though our eyes may tear

From prolonged observation of the water
In which we find the cruel
Transfiguration of cruel
Time, our adversary, and not a weak

One. From the clear water,
Our earliest mirror, we first suffer attacks
Of the spirit, those awful tears
In our self-conceptions whereby object

Is separated from subject, and object
Is found the lesser of the pair. A cruel
Division, and crucial, as it tears
Us away from ourselves. Weak

At first from such division, by further attacks
We grow weaker, and from the water
Rise angered, calling the water
A betrayer, and the distance from the object

Art: a length, an accounting, a tax
On imagination, which observes with cruel
Compassion our alter ego, our weak
Familiar shed wooden tears.

Totenlieder

Death cannot touch this music,
Terrible, inviolate as the sulphur sky,
Mastered in the throats of small-hearted thrushes.
These notes, cast down the dark corridor
As sparks cast down to ignite tinder,
Burn into the hearing. It is spring,
Corn grows in a gray field, a woman
With black hair wanders idly through the stalks,
Hearing the song she sings to herself
As if from great distance, and her heart
Turns to it, again and again, like a rock grinding
Against the sand in the sea. She sings against
The intrusions suffered by indifferent flesh
In the stiff air. She nears, again,
The stone wall which encloses the field,
And veers away, back into the pale saffron dust
Through which her feet stir. This field
Is not water, is not the lake, is not
The boat on the lake going down with
Her husband and daughter under a
Cloudless sky in which no wind stirs,
And no music. From the house, they can hear
Her singing, which is like shouting,
Shouting into the deaf light.

Medusae

Each night, on the rocky edge of sleep,
I feel you shudder against me,
Already slipping underwater
Where the first tentacles of dreams,
The evanescent jellyfish, brush
Against you.
          I dream of a wide sea
Where thousands of medusae
Float silently, each marking the currents
With its transparent grace.

          I dream of you
Transparent, your brain encased
In its clear shell, undulant,
Veined with pink, an umbrella-shape
That has risen and opened inside you.
Its tentacles trail down your spine
And wave in a shifting light.

I wake to the cold, trying to overcome
The liquid distance of the objects
In the room: the chair, the table,
The door. Your warmth spreads beside me.
I see your black hair a snaky tangle
On the pillow, and your features,
Familiar and composed.

Observing Whales through Binoculars

Fountains in a gray field,
Whales spout off the rough beach. A gray sky
Meets the gray sea in a vague horizontal.
A black flipper scythes the water

Beneath the gulls scattered
Through scarred lenses. No matter that
The wind registers upon a ruptured sea.
The ear records a near soundless

Tableau: only movements controlled
By the elements they move forth among.
Three blue figures watch from the white sand
And corn grass wavering

In a wavering air. Without binoculars,
We are diminished forms, figures
In a figurative scape. An orange-and-black dragger
Cuts through the short waves. The sky is an irruption

Of glamour into the material world.
We do not need language
To demonstrate the whales making their way
    north.
They are absorbed by their blue observers.

The Man in Pain

i

He awakens in a house, seiged by fields,
Where the furnace mills its grinding heat.
Huddling horses break from each other

As the ice lake cracks into a hundred
Islands. A dark-winged chorus calls
From match-stick trees. He knows the light

They know of. The ordinary morning arrives.
Like windows, the mirrors of the bathroom
Open into the same unexplored land

They closed on the night before, showing
The dull sky through a sliver of glass
Where a painter remembered what lay

Beyond the familiar face and introduced
The lead-lined air and beginnings of landscape.
There should be nothing more. Horses lope

To the blind side of their domain. The dog
Scratches at the door where cattle mouth
The muddy hay. A hunter crosses the fields

Bearing a bloody grouse. Wrenching open a window,
The man in pain finds crows strutting everywhere
In the wide yard, flapping their wide black wings.

ii
Because the temporal laws do not permit him
To shoot the crows bending their heavy bodies
Around the summer house, he is reduced

To leaving meat out for the flies.
To be a god, he cannot admire the insistence
Of their buzzing. For the carnivorous flowers

Lining the makeshift greenhouse, the flies
Will be meat: stored in a stone jar
They live out a thin existence on each other.

Even the minor deities cannot admire
The escape of an animal or the broken wall
Barring the pines from the fallow field.

They must maintain an independent existence,
Where to interefere is to damage the judgment
Of things. The flytraps close on the flies.

The hawk catches in its mechanical claws
A new meal. They devour one another
As if to hide from the inconstant light.

iii

The light that beats the rushes down
Is not the light of reason. What travels
The sky is the dark flock returning

By its unconscious celestial mechanics.
In a dull religious house, he seeks the basement
By flashlight, discovering the fixed

Eyes of a cat frozen to its corner. Beyond
The configurations of stored furniture,
It seems to stare toward an interstitial death.

On this day, the operations of the lungs
Squeeze blue. This house, this labyrinth
Of forgetful passages, is adventitious

And strange. The minor universe of animals
Has made it its center, and he has chased
The squirrels from the attic, the mice

From the walls, so nothing will be left
Over which to exercise a local influence.
Large tracks circle the house from the thicket.

In the steamy kitchen hangs a rusty ring
Of keys. The different doors
Open outward into an uncomfortable land.

Seventy-Six

Her dream rebuilt the packet ships, the port
No longer a port, its river silted
Shallow, the gray light dead and wrong, tilted
East on the horizon. Failing moonlight
Covers the wrinkled bed; the Fahrenheit
Thermometer reads normal. She can go
Home now. She clutches the portfolio
Of her novel, unfinished yet. 'I wrote
"The trout meander"—they don't. Do they?
        Your note
Cheered me *immensely*. Of course the plot is bad—
No theme. Three boys must drown fishing. I had
Two—your uncles. Boys I mean. Jacksonville
Is too warm for me. I prefer the hills
Of Cohasset—you remember. Write soon.
The fish—of course! They slither.' Afternoon,
A northern village, a northern river,
Snow on the salt grass. The birds form over
Long Point. Her uncle was an actor, not
Famous—played once to a real jury: not
Guilty, finally, but, career ruined,
He died in debt. Now she was sick—it rained—
And during this pneumonia played Camille,
Though not dying, not eating, getting well
With dramatic slowness. Writing in bed
Made her weak and mad; to honor the dead,
Her parents, depressed her. 'This depression
Makes me write,' she wrote. 'Voices in unison—
I hear them still—my parents, their old parents,
The whole aging lot. And now your success.
Your brothers will be rich—not you. Oh yes.

Not you. The novel lengthened, lengthened, got
In the way. Now I work on it in fits—
The climax is the storm of '98.
I cannot find the theme within the knots
Of prose. But, please, no advice. I know where
The theme should be.' In the pitch of weather,
When flooding took the family property.
The river broke a new mouth to the sea.

Three Lives

JOSEPH CONRAD

Hypnotic moon on black water, floating
Under a blank sky, no boat returning
To port tonight. Bodies in the water:
Images that interrupt the calm life
In murderous England, where only wheat
Moves like waves, or the rippling crowd in which
The anarchist lurks. Exile in the world,
He wrote these sure disasters out; they now
Have barged into a world beneath the world,
Where all hearts are bloody, all ignorance
Certain as greed. In the uneasy light
At morning, we anxiously remember
The tall palms breaking in the midnight storm,
Or the convulsions of disease and love.

CAMILLA, DAUGHTER OF METABUS

That a man trailed closely by murderers
Would unhorse at a rain-swollen river;
That he would lift up his infant daughter,
Cocoon her in cork bark and tie her fast
To his gnarled spear, then hurl her small body
Across the water; that she would become
A child of Diana: virgin huntress,
Horse soldier; that she would lead cavalry
Against Aeneas and his dark Trojans;
And that she would die through the treachery
Of a gritless man, a wound in the back,
Illustrate fate's suffocating embrace.
This mythology does not bother gods;
Each woman falls to a coward, a man.

A VALENTINE FOR MATTHEW ARNOLD

The Seas of Faith are full again with vain
Philosophies, empty orders of gods,
Demons of the mind and heart supplanting
The slow angers of love with hollow stares
And rhetoric. These are not days to love,
When the rare expectations of morning
Will be blackened by the shoddy evening.
Let us be faithless to one another.
The monarch butterflies now copulate
In the kitchen, bats bare their teeth against
The screens, and throatless songbirds rasp all night.
At dawn, armies of toads and frogs litter
The walks. All animals act cruelly
Toward each other. We are no different.

Mise en scène

If sleep is a curtain, what play does it drop on?
This dumb show, this ornamented silence
Rehearsed and returned to each night to exhaustion.
The night has blacked the windows again,
Jealous of its secrets. Clothed in your silence,
You wonder where to place Melancholy
So she appears to advantage, spoiling
Your entrance and savaging your lines.

We wait for each other to speak,
To walk barefoot across this stage of splinters,
Tentatively, without disturbing our numbed emotions
Sprawled in the stuffed chairs.
Like children, we wait for some outside deliverance,
Too uncertain to make the first move,
Second guessing, caught in the fourth act again,
Biding our time.
                    Somewhere, on an imaginary stage,
An angel swings in from the wings,
Flapping frantically, spilling feathers
And struggling against his brace.
It is the wrong angel. Take heart from this.
Any angel may teach us the lesson,
What tricks to perform to entertain sleep,
Our late and awaited visitor.

The Moth Disturbs the Night

It is late. The owls sleep. Moths lie stretched
    Against the screen, their eyes
Afire from the inside light that glows

    Duller as the daylight
Advances, from shrinking violet
    To a cornflower blue,
And overthrows the violent night
    With quiet heat. The wind
Stirs up the trees. From exhaustion my eyes burn,

    A long absence of sleep
Penetrating their white with a wild
    Red that tears, into which
Even emotions are soluble,
    Cannot dilute. The sea
May speak to me. I have learned its rare language

    Tonight. If only pain
Passed as quickly as winter's last storm
    Gives way to spring's demands,
Or could be rendered chemically
    Whole, as blue blood nearing
The patient lungs, or released to the open

    Air from an opened vein,
Turns red. From a dark wall, a moth has
    Fallen to the table.
Its head, brown feathers. Its banded wings,
    Smeared and diminutive
Wedges of slate. It seems recently mined from

Wet earth; it resembles
The black clay in the fields after rain.
With a clap of my hand
I could kill it. The luminescence
Of its muddied wings stays
Me. Such random unnatural artfulness,

Retained for protection
From predators or a convincing
Identification
In courtship, is as fragile as the
Tracery of blood in
My eyes or the cirrus on the horizon.

Qualities unmastered
By it keep it alive, as breath, or
Heartbeat, or pain do me.
It is not from the unknown that I
Salvage a comfort which
Allows me to survive the night. But I may

Not know myself. The night
Weakens again. The moth lies still on
The table. I may sleep.

Travel Report

Just before dawn, when the crows practice
Their four-noted alarm, sometimes managing
A brief chorus in unison, a last coolness
Leaves the skin and heat moves in to stay.
Equipped with ceiling fans of indifferent
Manufacture, the only hotel commands a view
Of the gray dirt, coarse as salt, merging
Unidentifiably with the yellow sky. At first
It seems a mistake to be here, and tourists
Line up at the information office, demanding
Explanations from a clerk who shrugs in sympathy.

Not even the guards care any longer
About immigrants who wander over this country's
Labyrinthine borders, but emigration is strictly
Controlled by bribe. The indigenous lizards
Dwell mostly underground and are losing their
Keen sight and smell, their violent colors.
Under the old rulers, a pantheon of deities
Was worshipped, but the real god is the sun,
Hereditary and ubiquitous. By afternoon
There is little to do except perfect the language,
Spoken slowly and with difficulty.

This is a turned land, where people flee
From contact with each other and love, like plague,
Is avoided, the contagion of contiguity.
None of the residents is anxious to leave, however,
And tourists after a month or two seem resigned
To their location, often giving up jobs and homes,
Sinking into this country's welcoming languor.
The only road leads toward smaller, hotter countries.

Ice

Men are walking on the harbor!
Secure in the physics of temperature,
They step from boat to lodged boat.

Under the fiery stars, cars play their headlights
Over a white continent. The bay is a land of floes,
And every twelve hours the tides

Lay up sheets of ice on the shore.
In a week they are piled as high as a man,
A dozen strata, histories of the tidal night.

And one morning, two days after warm weather,
The whole white shelf sinks into the sea,
Leaving raw sand and the angry waves.

What has kept us from falling?
Not winter's weird equilibrium.
Or earth drawing the reluctant feet

Down. Balance is the memory
Of the fall, before it happens.
Our inner charts are navigators' guesses:

White floes, flaws, flyaway islands.
Remnants of a vanished something.
The stories that mapped Viking explorers.

Or Frobisher's five men, captured by Eskimos,
A tribe that three centuries after
Remembered their release, the small boat

They built, the manner of their death.
Cold water, and England a long way.
We stay on land that holds us.

Or one morning walk out over the blue ice.

Dream of Dying

My friend's hands fall on me like leaves.
Covering my illness to a depth of compassion,
Relieving me of the burden of myself:

Their cool touch stills fever, stills
The impossible motion of anything real:
Mirrors, quilts, the annoying tick

Of the heart: full speed, it
Is traveling down a darker channel,
Uncharted, unmanned, toward some fantasy

Island populated by lives fevered like mine:
Or by creatures half-man, half-spirit,
Infused with the wish of being,

Acting some obscure play or dream
Of life: there is a field that men's throats
Bloodied, where the chemicals in their awkward

Bones hurried the harvest, their canteens
Rusted and were buried, their horses carted off
For meat. What rights have I retained

Against endings? I am ready to try drugs
There are no names for:
They will let me continue this dream

Of islands, and false harbors where
The ship slows to full stop
And the rough hands melt from my head.

The Man on the Bed

My grandfather was no honest man,
For honesty is of little use when a man,
By profession, sells kitchen gadgets
To people who will be hard-pressed recalling
The reason for their purchase. When I asked him
How he persuaded Midwest housewives to buy
His merchandise, he said he often had luck
With an anecdote of one sort or another.
He then told me a story he had found
Particularly good for entertainment.
'Once,' he would say to a customer,
'When I was on a long sales trip, my wife
Was sick, I later found out, with a cold
Or influenza, or a woman's complaint,
And was spending time in bed. One evening,
Clear for winter, she had gone to bed early,
Leaving the front door unlocked for a neighbor
Who had promised to see how she was.
My wife fell asleep, and sometime afterward awoke
Feeling disturbed. First she thought it was snowing,
But the night was clear and through
The oak branches she could see a great full moon.
She told me it seemed like a shining,
Whirling onion. It cast a shaft of light
Across her bed, so sharp she could see its edges
And reached to touch them. It was while she waved
Her hands in the moonlight that she heard a
    double breath
Her own breath traveling into the room, through
    the light,
Repeated. At first she was not frightened.
She breathed, heard the echoed breath, and
    breathed again.
She breathed more slowly, but each breath was repeated

Just as slowly, so she could not tell
If she were hearing some other person breathe, or if
The sounds which matched her breath
Were just some trick of the ear, as on a quiet day
Our voice, if we speak just loudly enough,
Will echo off the trees or houses near us.
It was then she saw a figure sitting
On the edge of the bed, beyond the moonlight.
She wondered why she had not seen it before,
Then realized that until her eyes had adjusted
To the surrounding darkness, she couldn't see
Further than the shaft of light.
She thought at first it was her neighbor,
Then realized this was a man.
She thought then that it was me, home early
From my trip, and so sat up and called, "John."
The man on her bed did not speak.
She thought perhaps I was daydreaming
And had not heard her.
She called the man again by my name.
He did not respond, and, realizing
That it was not her neighbor, nor was it me,
My wife began to become frightened.
She could not make out the man's features,
Only his shape against the wallpaper.
She was too frightened to move from the bed,
And too frightened to lie back on the pillow,
And so remained where she was, sitting up in bed,
In the moonlight, listening to them both breathe.
This was when the man leaned toward her
And said, in a very low voice,
"Don't worry. I will not hurt you."
It was then that she began to scream.
Even now, she cannot remember what happened

24

After that. Sometime later, she stopped screaming
And began crying, but by that time
The man was gone. She was still too scared
To move from the bed,
So she stayed and cried until she slept.
It was morning when she awoke, and,
Rembering all that had occurred the night before,
It was some time before she was able
To force herself from the bed and make sure
The house was hers again. Wrapped in her robe,
Armed with a pair of scissors, she searched each room,
Opening the closets and stooping under the tables,
Always afraid that she would come upon him.
Now here is the strangeness of the matter.
My wife thought that the man, if not a rapist,
Might have been a burglar or a bum, but nothing
Of value was missing, nor was there any less food
In the icebox than there had been the evening before.
And, when she went to the door to lock it,
She found that it was locked already.
The door she had left open the night before
Was locked now from the inside.
At this point she ran outside to her neighbors'
And refused to leave their house
Until I returned some two weeks later.
Now I do not know whether to believe my wife
Or not. When I am gone, my wife is a lonely woman,
And I'm inclined not to believe there
Was a strange man on her bed, but,
Even so, her fright was real.
I think she may have dreamed it all.
She may have wanted me home so badly
That she dreamed that I was home, but,
In the way of dreams, did not answer her

When she called my name. Or perhaps it was not me,
Perhaps the man she dreamed of, who frightened
        her so,
Was Death, I do not know.' And then slowly
My grandfather would add, 'Or even,
Perhaps, and I only think this late at night,
And usually when alone, and the night
Clear and strange like that night, perhaps it was
No dream, perhaps it was Death himself
Who sat upon her bed, and somehow she was so
        frightened
That he took pity on her,
And decided to leave her alone that time,
And come back again some other night.
Of course, in the daylight I'm as sane
As you or anyone, and don't tend
To believe that particular interpretation.
Still, I do not like to leave her alone
For too long, and so,' he would finish,
"That is why I would like to complete this trip
And return to her as soon as possible, and to that end
Might I interest you in the purchase
Of one of these handy conveniences?"

The Mantis

Now prisoners of summer's air,
We admire the polluted sunsets
Rising from Dulles. Two mantises
Mate in the backyard holly,

Thorned and wild. All one evening
I return to watch their passion.
By morning the male has vanished—
Eaten by his mate—

And the female disappears as I watch
Sacs of spiders hatch in a neighbor's fir.
Days later, the mantis returns
To attack the screen door,

Battering her head against the aluminum.
Like the children shouting all day
In the next house, I am fevered
By isolation. The closed backyards

Circumnavigate a court where
Spiders maneuver across the walls.
Monstrous crickets rub along
The living-room's mustard carpet:

There seems no way in. I let them go
Outdoors by the rows of black
Mailboxes. I find them again
Chewing grass seed in the metal shed,

Thumping inside the plastic bags.
Tonight the airport lights
Shake behind the cumulus. Inmates
Of the basement are laying eggs for spring.

A Portrait by Bellocq

One day even this transfigured flesh will shatter
Or burn, and its remains shower the dirt

Where motions freeze in a simple light
Whether or not the season submits to death.

This light, not simple or singular, divides
The self from the self, the portion

Which passes through it and moves beyond it
And lies down, and what is pictured forever,

Drawn into visionary circumstance, a profile
Against a shadowed door. How a submissive

Meter infects the heart is difficult to explain.
Why is difficult to remember. In every woman

There is a moment when the past precludes itself
From defeat or victory, and for you that moment

Came when you left behind the shallow season
Of the photographer and chose a future,

Not of fire or decay, but one that would
Lead there in its own slow fashion.

Tatiana Kalatschova

Only a woman of this measure
Suits the industry model.
Among the headless torsos she stands
Unyielding and calm as a perfect

Saint about to be burned, as they sew
The cloth around her bones
Unlike anyone else's bones,
Being noble, Russian, a measure

For all the dresses to be sewn
In her common size. When she models,
The designers become accustomed to the perfect
Blonde posture her body takes as it stands

In their dresses. She understands
The satisfaction in bones
That year to year perfect
Their proportions. Take her measure:

From it they have made mannequins, models
Named for a dead czar's daughter, who sewed
As her sisters and servants sewed
Rubies into pillows, and then were made to stand

In the basement to be bloodied by the model
Soldiers who poured acid on their bones.
This Tatiana dances to a different measure,
The hem and drape of perfect

Design. She need not perfect
The techniques of the peasant, to sew
Bolt and bolt of cloth without measure,
To harvest the corn when it stands,

To find in a chicken the bones
Thin as the bones of a model.
But any woman, whether a model
To industry or blessed with imperfect

Proportions, knows that skin will weaken her bones.
When the czar is murdered, let it not end so
Quickly, she might say, unless she understands
That silence is itself a measure.

The Lizard in His Medium

Sly, like the French horn's plunge,
Soft, like a child's whisper, the forked tongue
Marks temperature, measures the wind's
Currents. The tongue knows no true path.

The reptile's gentle lisp, his sinister
Manners, his scale coat, his frangible tail:
What will he whisper when the lights go out?
How will he know our saurian taste?

'Hish-hish' washes over this. Was there
An eye more clear, more clever? He has
The leopard's hunger. The flap ears close.
He walks and walks.

He lives in the observation of the moment's
Flicker, the watched ascendancy of night:
It is the sharp minute in which he breathes.
To live beneath things supernal,

In that muted harmony that is eating and taking,
Taking and giving back, his composition of pause,
Where time is a weight and moment nothing.
The absent dark: his movement is silence.

The sand is only a temporary home.

Maelstrom

Vain, stupid, brutal to myself,
Attracted to a younger man
No brighter—but no hunger can
Drive the young lover from my dreams.
Eyes shut, I wash my hair in steam
From the ancient tub, its claw feet
Clutching balls that drive its weight
Into the marble floor and zone
A rectangular space of stone
Where my mirror reflects its bottom.
The dirty windows load with flies
Mingling under a darkened sky
Where the weakened day suffers a breeze
To sweep us into night. I ease
Myself over the tub and pour
Warm water through my lathered hair
Until the drain sucks with froth.

I turn the ivory handles off
When the flies lurch against the screens
And windows slam through three rooms—rain:
Not a shower but the maelstrom,
The world, alive with water, comes
Down with the sightless force of dream.
The word is Dutch for grinding stream.
Everywhere its wheels of water
Pull us under, through downtown
Deserted streets, from underground
Cafés to the skeletal sky.
I lock the windows against the air.
The room calms. In a darkened chair,
A towel around my head, I sit down
To watch the guilty poplars drown.

The man I sleep with wants no child.
Though my sisters foster mild
Fears for me, they prepare for years
Of bearing. Why do I despair
The ignorance of love? Our parents
Want children to ornament
Their deaths. Our own deaths rise, clearer
Than that perishable mirror
History, and I find myself drawn
To pregnant, nervous girls. While
They thicken, I watch their juvenile
Breasts. Invisible children feed,
Wanting the chance of flesh.
                              Must
We choose as well what chooses us?
I don't know. You have been away.
We should end these fictions and live
Alone, if distance can forgive
Our love, our love its loss, and words
Their failure. What we have endured
Becomes no child. Heirs to each other,
Forbidden like sister and brother,
The tree will not blossom, the fly
Cannot breed. Despite the aging sky
And shreds of storm that scour the air
I must leave to meet your plane. Here
The ground lights up with stars of rain,
An image too pretty to last.

We Abandon the Gods on Our First Evening Together

We leave the theater and walk the blocks
To the bus, when it begins to rain.
We are caught in the open.
'Rain,' you say, 'is the tears of the gods
We have abandoned.' If only
This were Hollywood and your words,
Thus spoken, would cue the union men
On the kliegs and release us to the laughter
Of the dry studio workmen.

'I'm cold,' you say, and so am I.
I ask about your family,
Though their health is of no interest to me,
I ask your opinion of the movie, and I ask
About other forms of weather
In which you might have been caught and
        which might,
I hope, have been worse.

I look across the street
At the pawn shops and family businesses
Verging on failure. It all seems
So ordinary, and even you,
In the glare of the streetlight and in your impatience.
Begin to lose your fascination.
My skin is absorbing water, creating
A private inland sea. The drops
On my face feel like tears, and if
There are gods, they have abandoned us
To the rain. The bus turns the corner
And arrives.
                At my apartment, you undress,
Lost in your thoughts, and call the rain

34

A mysterious curtain of beads. Had I
More courage, I would argue. I hear it
As a series of slamming doors, the preludes
To scenes that have not begun.

An Ode

When weather ripens
Our intractable hearts, and the air
        Loses the gray
Soot and sulphur discharged
        By the cities,
And the small victims participate
        In the general
Well-being, so the squirrels in the
        Hunter's sack
Harmonize with the unapproachable sky,
        Then we should
Watch with care for signs of decline,
        Early portents
Of discontent that omen freeze and fall,
        The cold snap
That wipes out summer's gain; whether
        Real or imagined
Or some arbitrary mixture of the true
        And fantastic,
Like the quiet clerk who lives for weekends
        As a svelte
Transvestite, such moments of wariness balance
        Our expectation
That all will be right or pure or good
        Always, and
Argues an appropriate lesson: to find bad luck
        Necessary—
The knife that opens the child's hand,
        The telephone call
From the adulterer, the fracture of bone
        When the debtor
Is caught by the loan shark's implacable
        Heavy. These
Destroy, but their good does not end there.

Sheep

Where sheep floated in
One autumn from a stormless sea,
The sand cliffs wash down to flat shore.

These loose cargoes,
Like everything the sea returns,
Were put to work. Who understood their

Difficult journey? Their lanoline bodies
Bore them up, sailing in
Like men-of-war from outlandish waters.

Unsalvageable hulks block
A harbor where rocks dagger the water,
Bottles labeled with algae follow

String currents from Scotland.
All winter, stories come up
The hidden river, of Revolutionary ships

That on dark nights duck British raiders,
Seeming to sail along shore
Then disappearing into solid coast.

The foghorns fire their sporadic shells.
Like dragons' teeth, broken headstones
Seed the sailors' graveyard,

The sheep pasture, cenotaphs
For men who sailed a visible horizon
And vanished from view.

The Misbegotten

Your face smiles in the dark glass.
All day you have been
The shadow at my shoulder, the breath
At my ear in the ignorant calm. The leaves
Give up. The day gives up
And the light shrinks to the low planet
Out across the water.
                    Now the moon
Has broken a vein and blinks,
Half-closed and bloody.

Brother, brother, you are a jealous god
Of memory. For days when you slid
Into my dreams, you were a sister
Or a swan, like the swan I saw
Midsummer, out on the dark waves,
Too confused to come in.

Now the stars flower in the glass.
I thought that windows gave us safety
From the night, the way
The sun's violence is turned
By a common sky. Tonight they all are mirrors.

She Arrives at Night, Unexpected

Your visit does not disturb me,
I am like an oak, you—
                              A recurrent vine?
You have changed little.
Your child has worn you little.
This apple reminds me of your heart.
Have you read the papers?
                              Not recently.
The war lingers
Like a wound too wide to stitch. Talk!
Our common enemy is silence. There lurks
No hidden order. What was obscure
We obscured. What was obscene we
Made obscene.
                              Have you seen my friend?
When I last saw him,
A half-grown beard covered his cheeks
Like rust. He gnawed the rind of an orange.
'Are you still writing?' he asked.
'Most of us have given it up.'
My poetry *has* given me trouble.
It does not ... communicate.
I write things into extinction.

Your blond hair is still like the sun
After rain. You probably still hide your teeth
When you laugh. See?
Nothing changes. He wrote me later:
'No man can be precisely
What he wants. That is the first
Secret. The rest beware of.
And beware fools of all orders.
Much I cannot express. Yours.'
                              I can't understand him.

You are concerned with the detail
Of life. He is not there?
When did he leave you?
                    Weeks. I have been alone.
I pierced your body, never your heart.
The delight we unleashed
Was a private violence.
When I kiss the lips of the poster on my wall,
I injure no one. I did not expect you.
Your breath is still pleasant—
We touch, but cannot be near.